MW00573095

What Makes Objects Move?

 HOUGHTON MIFFLIN HARCOURT

PHOTOGRAPHY CREDITS: COVER (bg) ©GUSTOIMAGES/Science Photo Library/ Getty Images; 3 (b) ©Stocktrek Images, Inc./Alamy Images; 4 (b) ©David Madison/Stone/Getty Images; 5 (t) ©alens/Shutterstock; 6 (b) © Brand X Pictures/Getty Images; 7 (t) ©GUSTOIMAGES/Science Photo Library/Getty Images; 10 (l) ©Image Source/Corbis, (r) ©ronstik/Shutterstock; 12 (b) ©Germanskydiver/Shutterstock; 13 (b) ©Science Source/Photo Researchers/ Getty Images; 14 (l) ©Ilene MacDonald/Alamy Images; 14 (r) ©Ilene MacDonald/Alamy Images; 16 (b) ©Brand X Pictures/Getty Images; 17 ©tka4u4a/Shutterstock; 18 (b) ©Alpha and Omega Collection/Alamy Images; 19 (t) ©Photodisc/Getty Images; 22 (b) ©Patrick Semansky/AP Images

Printed in Mexico

ISBN: 978-0-544-07317-3

6 7 8 9 10 0908 21 20 19 18 17 16

4500608014   A B C D E F G

Be an Active Reader!

 Look at these words.

position	speed	acceleration
motion	velocity	force

 Look for answers to these questions.

Are you moving?

How do you define motion?

What are some types of motion?

How can you tell if something is really moving?

How are changes in motion measured?

What is acceleration?

What are rates of acceleration?

Which accelerates faster?

What causes objects to accelerate?

When doesn't an object accelerate?

How many forces act on an object?

What is the force called gravity?

What is friction?

How does magnetism make objects move?

How is motion detected?

Are you moving?

"If I'm sitting still at my desk, I'm not moving. If I get up and walk around, I am moving." This might seem obvious. It may even sound like a silly thing to say. But let's take a closer look. When you are sitting still, only parts of you are really not moving. Your eyelids blink, and your blood cells move through your blood vessels. Additionally, your chair and the whole Earth on which you sit are moving through outer space! So, you're always moving somehow. The question really is, "Moving in relation to what?"

Every object in the solar system is continually moving in relation to another object.

How do you define "motion"?

In order to know if you're moving or not, you have to know where you started! In other words, you have to know your position. Position is the place where something is located in relation to a nearby object or place. For example, you may be sitting in a chair. If so, that's your position.

Motion is what happens when you move. Motion is a change in position. For example, if you get up from a chair, you are in motion. You have changed your position.

This racing car is changing its position.

A pitcher throws a curveball. The motion includes upward, downward, forward, and sideways directions.

What are some types of motion?

Objects can move in any direction. They can also change direction, speed up, or slow down. They can move in a straight line forward or backward, turn a corner, or move in a curve. They can also continue to move in just one direction.

Different types of motion can work together. Think about what happens when a baseball pitcher throws a curveball. His arm whips toward home plate and releases the ball forward. At the same time, the ball rises in the air a few centimeters. Then it dips a few centimeters. It has moved upward and downward as well as forward. Also, the twist of the pitcher's wrist moves the ball sideways. The ball is moving in four directions at once. No wonder it's hard to hit!

How can you tell if something is really moving?

You've learned that you never move by yourself. You always move in relation to another object. This is completely logical, when you think about it. After all, how would you know you were changing position if you didn't have anything to which to compare your position?

Imagine that you're an astronaut in a spacecraft in deep space. There are no planets, stars, or other objects nearby. How would you know whether your spacecraft was moving? It would be impossible.

In order to know that you're moving, you need a reference point—an object to which you can compare your position. If you were on a sailing ship coming into a harbor, your reference point would be the dock.

The astronauts in this spacecraft have no reference point to check, so they can't tell whether the spacecraft is moving or not.

The man in the picture is moving. The background is the frame of reference.

A reference point is a single location. You use reference points in your own movements. Suppose you're walking to get through the school door before the bell rings. You check to see how close you are to the door. The door is your reference point.

Sometimes you use a large background rather than a single reference point. A large background used as a reference point is called a frame of reference.

Using a frame of reference is helpful when you are comparing the movement of more than one object. For example, at a swim meet, you can see all the swimmers moving within the frame of reference of the pool.

How are changes in motion measured?

You're riding in a car at a speed of 80 kilometers per hour (km/hr). Speed is the measure of an object's change in position during a certain amount of time. So, the position of the car will change by 80 kilometers every hour. Suddenly, a car passes you on the left. That car is moving at a speed that is faster than you. It's traveling at a speed that is greater than 80 kilometers per hour. Since its speed is greater than yours, it will cover a greater number of kilometers each hour.

Speed is a simple way to measure just how fast something is moving. If you know the direction of the moving object, you can also know its velocity. Velocity adds direction to speed.

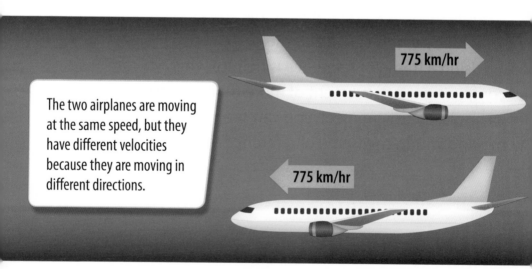

775 km/hr

775 km/hr

The two airplanes are moving at the same speed, but they have different velocities because they are moving in different directions.

Here's how to measure the speed of an object traveling in a straight line. Suppose a caterpillar is crawling on a branch. Put a meterstick or metric ruler on the branch. Place the zero mark at the point where you first start observing the caterpillar. With a watch or stopwatch, check the time. How far along the meterstick does the caterpillar move in 1 minute? In 10 minutes?

You can figure out how fast the caterpillar is moving by using this formula: Speed equals distance divided by time. Suppose the caterpillar went 6 centimeters (cm) in 6 minutes (min). If you divide 6 cm by 6 min, your answer is 1 cm/min (6 cm ÷ 6 min = 1 cm ÷ min).

Use this table to think of questions about animal distances and speeds, such as, "How long could it take a horse to run a kilometer?"

Animal Top Speeds	
homing pigeon	150 km/hr
cheetah	110 km/hr
hummingbird	100 km/hr
horse	80 km/hr
jackrabbit	70 km/hr
deer	65 km/hr
grizzly bear	55 km/hr

What is acceleration?

You know that the speed of an object moving in a particular direction is its velocity. What if the direction changes? For example, you're walking down the street at 5 km/hr (3 mph), and you turn the corner. You have changed your direction. What if your speed also changes? As you're walking, you might go slower or faster. Any of these actions is called acceleration. Acceleration is any change in the speed or direction of an object's motion.

You may have thought that *acceleration* just means "speeding up." Acceleration is any change in velocity. An object accelerates when it speeds up, slows down, or changes direction.

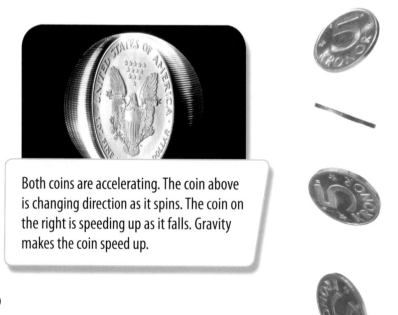

Both coins are accelerating. The coin above is changing direction as it spins. The coin on the right is speeding up as it falls. Gravity makes the coin speed up.

In science, deceleration is negative acceleration.

One form of acceleration that you might be familiar with occurs when a car starts moving when a red light turns green. The car accelerates until it reaches the speed of traffic. When the next light turns red and the car slows down, the slowing down is called deceleration. Deceleration is just another form of acceleration!

A car has a gas pedal and a brake. Pushing down on the gas pedal, which is sometimes called the accelerator, makes the car go faster. The brake is also a kind of accelerator, only it slows the car down. Even the steering wheel is a kind of accelerator, because it can change the direction of the motion.

What are rates of acceleration?

Acceleration occurs when an object falls to the ground. This is because the object's speed changes. Picture a skydiver who has just dived from an airplane. The farther the skydiver falls, the faster he or she falls. The increase in the speed is the rate of acceleration.

An object falling through the air with no wind accelerates at a constant rate—9.8 meters per second per second. This number is written as 9.8 m/s^2. You can also say meters per second squared.

acceleration of a skydiver in free fall

Which accelerates faster?

Now suppose that two objects are falling side by side. They are the same shape, but one is heavier than the other. One is a baseball and the other is a bowling ball. You hold one in each hand and drop them at the same time. Which will reach the ground first?

The baseball and the bowling ball will hit the ground at the same time! Objects falling to Earth accelerate at the same rate, no matter what their weight is. You already know that the rate is 9.8 m/s^2.

This startling fact was discovered by the Italian scientist Galileo Galilei in about 1590. Before Galileo, many people believed that heavier objects fall faster.

Galileo Galilei (1564–1642) is sometimes called "the father of modern science."

What causes objects to accelerate?

An object accelerates when something either pushes it or pulls it. Something that pushes or pulls an object is called a force. A push or pull can go up, down, forward, backward, or in other directions.

A pull moves an object in the direction of the force. A push moves the object away from the force. When you pull a door open, you are applying a force. The door moves toward you. When you push the door closed, you are applying a force that moves it away.

Forces are what make objects start up, speed up, slow down, or stop. No motion occurs without a force.

If you pull or push an object, you are the force!

When doesn't an object accelerate?

If an object is accelerating when it is starting up, speeding up, slowing down, or changing direction, when isn't it accelerating? There are two times when an object is not accelerating. One is when it is standing still. The other is when it is moving at a constant speed in an unchanging direction.

Think back to the definition of acceleration. Acceleration is a change in velocity. If the speed is steady and the direction remains the same, then the velocity isn't changing. Therefore, no acceleration is taking place.

This boy is running but not accelerating. He's going straight in one direction at a constant speed.

How many forces act on an object?

Does only once force at a time act upon an object? No. In most cases, several forces are acting upon an object at every moment. Think about what happens when you ride a bicycle. One force is pushing you forward, speeding you up. Another force is pushing backward, making sure that you don't speed up forever. Another force is keeping the bicycle on the ground. Other forces are holding it up, keeping it balanced.

Even the forward movement is complicated. When the wheels turn forward, they are actually exerting a backward push against the road. When that happens, the road creates an equally strong force in the opposite direction. The force of the road is what pushes you forward. You actually move forward by pushing backward!

When the wheels push backward against the road, the force of the road pushes the wheels forward.

Without gravity, every object on Earth would float away.

What is the force called gravity?

As a bike moves forward, another force keeps it on the ground. This force is gravity. Gravity is the force that attracts two objects to each other. All objects have gravity. The more mass the object has, the more gravity it exerts on other objects. The closer two objects are to each other, the more gravity they exert on each other.

The gravity you're most familiar with is Earth's gravity. It's what keeps everything on this planet from flying away. Earth is very large, compared to the objects on it, so it might seem that Earth is the only object exerting gravity. However, while Earth is exerting gravity upon you, you are exerting gravity upon Earth. And all the nearby objects are exerting gravity on one another.

What is friction?

Another important force that acts throughout the universe is friction. Friction, the force that acts on objects rubbing together, opposes motion.

Imagine walking along a sandy or gravelly road and noticing that the ground catches the soles of your shoes. When that happens, you are noticing friction. The soles of your shoes and the ground are rubbing together.

Friction doesn't just occur when you are walking. It's present whenever two moving objects are in contact with each other. Friction slows the speed of objects. It also creates heat.

When two objects rub together, friction changes kinetic energy into heat energy. That's why rubbing two sticks together makes fire.

Even this smooth ice has some friction. Without it, this skater could not stop.

The smoother an object is, the less friction it exerts on other objects. The rougher it is, the more friction it exerts. The less friction there is, the farther and faster an object can move. A carpeted floor provides a lot of friction, so much that you could never slide across it in your socks. You could slide across a smooth wood or tile floor. You could slide even more easily—and farther—on a polished floor than an unpolished floor.

Friction may not help you slide quickly on floors, but without friction you wouldn't be able to slow down and stop. Without friction, car brakes would not work. Stopping a bicycle would be almost impossible without friction.

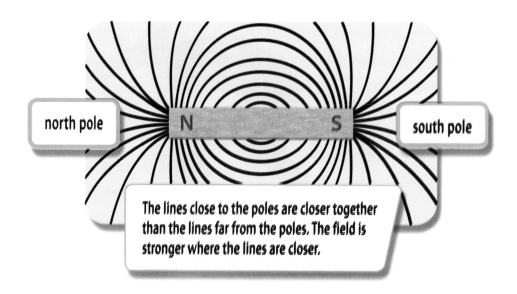

north pole

N   S

south pole

The lines close to the poles are closer together than the lines far from the poles. The field is stronger where the lines are closer.

How does magnetism make objects move?

Another force that can make objects move is magnetism. Magnetism is a force that can attract objects without touching them by setting up a magnetic field.

A magnet contains two ends called poles. One is north; the other is south. The magnetic field is stronger near the two poles. When the magnetic field interacts with a magnetic object (usually one made of iron or nickel), it exerts a force on the object.

Two magnetic fields can interact with one another. If the two poles are different—one north and one south—they attract. If the two poles are both south or north, the magnets will repel one another.

Scientists show forces in magnetic fields by drawing lines. A quick experiment will also show these magnetic fields. Put a magnet on a piece of paper. Sprinkle iron filings on the paper. Watch as the iron filings line themselves up with the lines of magnetic force!

Some materials are attracted to magnets, and some aren't. Iron and nickel are the most common magnetic metals. When an object made of iron or nickel enters a magnetic field, the atoms in the object line up toward the poles. The metal object is magnetized. That means that the object itself becomes a magnet. A pole on the object will be attracted to the opposite pole on the magnet. The object will move toward the magnet.

A student sprinkled iron filings around a magnet to see the lines of magnetic force.

How is motion detected?

Sometimes it's important to know where, when, and how fast objects are moving. One tool that tracks motion is radar. Radar sends sound waves at an object. The sound waves bounce off the object and then back to their source. Changes in the waves show how the object changes position.

Aircraft controllers use radar to keep track of planes in the sky. Police use radar to check the speed of cars. In baseball, radar measures the speed of a pitched ball.

Magnetic devices can detect motion, too. A compass needle is made of magnetized metal. The compass tracks the direction you move by responding to the magnetic north pole of the earth. No matter which direction you move, the compass will always point north.

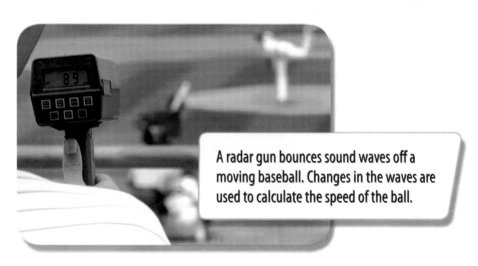

A radar gun bounces sound waves off a moving baseball. Changes in the waves are used to calculate the speed of the ball.

Design a Friction Experiment

Plan and carry out an experiment to find out more about friction. Use the following materials: two or more pairs of shoes and one or more different floor or ground surfaces. Compare the friction of the soles of the shoes and the floor or ground surfaces. Make sure to ask a question at the beginning, form a hypothesis, carry out your observations, record your data, and arrive at a conclusion.

Write about Friction and Gravity

Look for examples of friction and gravity in real life. Write down at least five examples of each. For each example, write a sentence or two describing the effects of the force. Are the effects useful or harmful?

Glossary

acceleration [ak•sel•er•AY•shuhn] Any change in the speed or direction of an object's motion.

force [FOHRS] A push or a pull.

motion [MOH•shuhn] A change of position of an object.

position [puh•ZISH•uhn] The location of an object in relation to a nearby object or place.

speed [SPEED] The measure of an object's change in position during a certain amount of time.

velocity [vuh•LAHS•uh•tee] The speed of an object in a particular direction.